AF425877

Declarations for My Sons

Denise N. Fyffe

DECLARATIONS FOR MY SONS

Jamaica Pen

www.theislandjournal.com

Acknowledgement

I would like to extend my appreciation to my Lord and Savior Jesus Christ, who has bestowed on me, many gifts; without Him none of this, is possible. This is dedicated to and stands as the foundation for my children's lives.

Denise N. Fyffe.

Prayer

Lord Jesus,

We thank you for your great gift. I pray that the hearts, minds, spirits and souls of the men, and women reading this book will be opened to the influence, love, word and leading of the Holy Spirit. I declare that they will receive divine favor from you, God, and that miracles will flow into their lives. I declare grace, mercy, spiritual power, and love in their bloodlines. I decree that they and their children will come to know you in full as their Lord and Savior. Let thy will be done and let thy kingdom come on earth as it is in heaven.

In Jesus name, Amen

Declarations for My Sons

Introduction

Declarations are assertions. The dictionary defines the word as a formal or explicit statement or announcement. In other words, it is a message, pronouncement, or proclamation. It carries the same weight as an oath or contract and can be considered a legally binding statement.

In our world, the British monarchy or even our governments, make proclamations very often; it is a part of their duty. These statements are obeyed and those who disobey are punished. People obey proclamations. In the spiritual realm, when we make a declaration, it must be obeyed. God honors our word and our decrees.

It says in Job 22:28 (KJV),

"Thou shalt also decree a thing, and it shall be established unto thee: and the light shall shine upon thy ways."

Demons and angels will also heed our declarations unless the divine will of Almighty God overrules it.

If you are like me, your interest is piqued when you hear prophets, pastors or bishops in the church making proclamations and they start with, "I decree and declare" such and such. Why is that? You might have also heard customs agents or immigration officers ask travellers in an airport, "Do you have anything to declare?"

When you declare something, you 'make it known'. When you make a decree, it is 'a statement of truth that carries the authority of a court order.' Therefore, it is effectively a tool that will cause things to manifest in both the spiritual and physical realm.

As children of God, Christians, we ought to make pronouncements over our lives. We are taught that as sons and daughters of the kingdom, heirs to the royal priesthood of Jesus Christ, we should make declarations and decrees. It is a way in which to exercise our will/authority and cause our purpose for a thing to be made manifest.

But, we should be careful that whatever we say, must be in accordance with the will of God.

God's will must always take precedence in our lives, but how can we be sure that we are following his will.

Easy, read the bible.

All scripture, references God's will. Therefore, it is more effective when we pair our declarations with the word of God. For example, Isaiah 53:5 states that *"… by your stripes I am already healed."*

A fitting declaration would be:

> *"I decree and declare that I am walking in health. I am healed according to the word of God found in Isaiah 53:5 (NKJV), which says "But He was wounded for our transgressions, He was bruised for our iniquities; the chastisement for our peace was upon Him, and by His stripes we are healed." I will prosper and live in health all my life, in Jesus name amen.*

Declarations are an exercise in the prophetic. You are speaking things into being, as we often say.

Contrary to what many believe, it is not only the prophet or those with a prophetic gifting can prophesy. It is all those who are filled with the Holy Spirit and have been given the gifts of the Spirit. Once we acknowledge and operate in the power and authority that Jesus Christ has given us, we can prophesy and so we can make prophetic declarations.

An attitude adjustment is also recommended.

We cannot make declarations like kings and queens, one second, and then the next, we continue with a defeatist mindset.

No, no! Our walk, our talk and our attitude must be bold.

We must act like we have already received what we asked for. Why? Remember, I stated earlier that what we declare happens first in the spiritual realm and then it manifests in the physical.

If you adopt a defeatist approach in the physical, your declarations might be nullified in the spiritual. Keep in mind that demons are always at work to steal the gifts that God has given us.

So, be bold! Enter into His gates with thanksgiving. Praise God!

Now that you are walking boldly, how about we exercise our new found gift for our children.

You don't have children?

Do not worry; declarations also work for those things, which have not yet manifested in the physical, remember? You can make prophetic declarations for every one of your children, grandchildren, children's children's children; every person who will be from your lineage.

Proverbs 18:21 (NKJV) states that, *"Death and life are in the power of the tongue, and those who love it will eat its fruit."*

Therefore, let us boldly declare good things into the lives of our ancestors, so that God's will shall reign supreme, even before conception. Fortresses shall be made, and your children will not depart from the protection therein.

God bless you.

In the beginning was the Word

While working on this book, I read '*The Man Who Talked with Angels*' a book by Sharon White. She was the daughter of Pastor Roland Buck, author of '*Angels on Assignment*.'

If you can, get a copy of these books and read them, I believe, you will never be the same.

In one of the chapters, it recounts a conversation between the angel Gabriel and Pastor Buck. Gabriel was explaining that he was there in the Holy of Holies with God when Zechariah was tending to the temple. He told Zechariah about the birth of John.

When I read, Luke 1:15 (KJV) my heart leapt with joy.

Here was proof for my declarations for my children, that they be filled with the spirit and speak in tongues, even from the womb; it was biblical. "*... He'll be filled with the Holy Spirit from the moment he leaves his mother's womb...*"

This was also God's urging to me.

It was time to continue working on this project that I had started year's end, 2015.

Declaration:

I declare and decree that according to Luke 1:14-17, my sons and daughters, shall bring their parents "... joy and gladness; and many shall rejoice at their birth. For they shall be great in the sight of the Lord, and shall drink neither wine nor strong drink; and they shall be filled with the Holy Ghost, even from their mother's womb. And many of your children on this earth,

God, shall they turn to the Lord their God. And they shall go before him in the spirit and power of Elias, to turn the hearts of the fathers to the children, and the disobedient to the wisdom of the just; to make ready a people prepared for the Lord."

Throughout this book, I will share many declarations. Please join me in saying them boldly and out loud, speaking them into the physical and spiritual realm. You may also choose to meditate on them, jointly with the respective bible verses referenced.

Prayer:

Oh Lord God, I declare and decree that the 'Declarations for My Sons', have a biblical foundation. They shall be rooted and grounded in the Word and they shall be divinely inspired by the Holy Spirit. This book will be a door for the Holy Spirit to rain down kingdom blessings on the sons and daughters of God; in Jesus name.

The Bible says in John 1:1-4 (KJV), that *"In the beginning was the Word, and the Word was with God, and the Word was God. The same was in the beginning with God. All things were made by him; and without Him was not anything made that was made. In Him was life; and the life was the light of men."*

Nothing can be separate from the Word of God and live.

The Word made manifest was Christ Jesus and it is on this foundation that all Christian sentiment, teaching and wisdom must stand. A popular song lyric, '... on Christ the solid rock I stand, all other ground is sinking sand, all other ground is sinking sand.' Therefore:

I declare that this book's foundation is Jesus Christ. It will not stray from the teachings of the bible and as such you will see many chapter and verse references. As such, the power of the Holy Spirit will drive this book to many nations, many lands, many homes, many families. It will be the catalyst to break generational curses and demonic strongholds in the lives of God's people.

As you consistently make these declarations, do not be surprised if you see supernatural manifestations in your homes and children. When God is on assignment, everything must change. He says that when you use His words, His promises, the only answer is yes and amen. This is stated in 2 Corinthians 1:20 (KJV) *"For all the promises of God in him are yea, and in him Amen, unto the glory of God by us."*

This is necessary so that the declarations you speak over your family's life, will stand the bombardment from the enemy, even to the 12th generation, even to eternity.

Who Did It First?

In this chapter, we will examine those principal characters in the bible that practiced blessing or making declarations over their children's lives.

We will examine the declarations themselves and the outcome. For how else should we proceed and be successful? If we do not look back and examine the template provided by not only the kings, princes, and generals; but also, the divine template passed down by Yahweh.

God

G od is the author and finisher of our faith. He leads by example. Genesis 9 contains one of the first declarations of a father, over the lives of his children. Here we see that God pronounced a blessing over Noah and his sons, after the flood. He also gave them a sign of His covenant.

This is the rainbow.

We see this in the sky when it rains. So, next time it rains, look up and admire this phenomenon, because the covenant God made is extended to you. You are a descendant of Noah through Abraham.

Then God blessed Noah and his sons and told them, "Be fruitful and multiply. Fill the earth. All the animals of the earth, all the birds of the sky, all the small animals that scurry along the ground, and all the fish in the sea will look on you with fear and terror. I have placed them in your power.

... Then God told Noah and his sons, "I hereby confirm my covenant with you and your descendants.

Then God said, "I am giving you a sign of my covenant with you and with all living creatures, for all generations to come. I have placed my rainbow in the clouds. It is the sign of my covenant with you and with all the earth. When I send clouds over the earth, the rainbow will appear in the clouds, and I will remember my covenant with you and with all living creatures.

Never again will the floodwaters destroy all life. When I see the rainbow in the clouds, I will remember the eternal covenant between God and every living creature on earth."

*Then God said to Noah, "Yes, this rainbow is the sign of the covenant I am confirming with all the creatures on earth." –
Gen 9:1-2, 8, 9, 12-17 (NLT)*

God's covenant with Noah has stood for many generations, thousands of years. We can rest assured that the whole earth will never be destroyed by flood again. Yes, there has been wide scale destruction, by hurricanes, typhoons, floods, mudslides, and tsunamis in diverse places. Millions of people have lost their lives. Nonetheless, we have always bounced back. Cities rebuild and life moves on.

Noah

Shortly after the flood, Noah made his first declaration over his children. He planted a vineyard, and then later he made wine from the grapes and became drunk. Ham happened upon his father naked and went to his older brothers, who wisely did not look on their father's nakedness and covered him.

When Noah revived, he made declarations over his sons, but cursed Ham's son, Canaan.

> *When Noah woke up from his stupor, he learned what Ham, his youngest son, had done. Then he cursed Canaan, the son of Ham: "May Canaan be cursed! May he be the lowest of servants to his relatives." Then Noah said, "May the Lord, the God of Shem, be blessed, and may Canaan be his servant! May God expand the territory of Japheth! May Japheth share the prosperity of Shem, and may Canaan be his servant." - Gen 9:24-26 (NLT)*

Noah's declaration was a curse. It was a judgment made against Ham, for his grave error. As such, the children of Ham and their generation have suffered greatly for the sins of their father. Please understand that it is not according to God's template to speak curses over our children. Many parents are quick to curse their children, rather than praise, bless and constructively guide them. Oftentimes, they do so in anger.

This should not be. It is in extreme cases, where a judgment must be declared. If God were like man, our whole generation would not have gotten to the embryonic stage. However, thank God for grace, mercy, and the sacrifice of Jesus Christ.

The heart of men can be easily misled by anger. That is why the bible stipulates in Proverbs 18:21 (NKJV) that *"Death and life are in the power of the tongue, and those who love it will eat its fruit."*

In Psalms 34:13 (KJV), it states that you should *"Keep your tongue from evil, and your lips from speaking guile."* The tongue is a mighty sword, and we must wield it with wisdom and responsibility, else the wound inflicted could devastate our own children for many generations.

1 Peter 3:9 *"Do not repay evil with evil or insult with insult. On the contrary, repay evil with blessing, because to this you were called so that you may inherit a blessing."*

Let's take a closer look at Ham's descendants, which included Babylon, Assyria, Nineveh, and Egypt. These were great civilizations. The Babylonians and Egyptians were permitted by God to enslave the people of Israel. Canaan's descendants did not fare well as time progressed. They were known for their perversion and idol worshipping. The Canaanites not only became enemies of the Israelites; it was Canaan's direct descendants who populated the areas of and surrounding Sodom and Gomorrah.

Do you recall the fire, brimstone, and hailstorm that utterly wiped Sodom and Gomorrah off the map? God also ordered the Canaanites destruction at the hands of the Israelites. Because of the demonic strongholds and generational curses found in these people, God warned the Israelites not to marry them. However, the Israelites disobeyed. This brought judgment on the people of Israel.

So, you see, Noah's declarations were effective and powerfully impacted the lives of Canaan's descendants. Even though he traditionally declared less for the younger sibling, later you will see, where Jacob reverses this practice.

Abraham

Abraham was special in the sight of God. He was a godly man, who sought after God. Yahweh declared a blessing that would emanate throughout Abraham's heirs and their generation.

> *The Lord had said to Abram, "Leave your native country, your relatives and your father's family and go to the land that I will show you. I will make you into a great nation. I will bless you and make you famous, and you will be a blessing to others. I will bless those who bless you and curse those who treat you with contempt. All the families on earth will be blessed through you."*
> *- Genesis 12: 1- 3 (NLT)*

Abraham was obedient and left his father's country. He had different trials but continued to travel until he settled in the hill country of the land of Canaan. Because of his obedience and fairness towards Lot, God added to his blessing.

> *And the Lord said to Abram, after Lot had separated from him: "Lift your eyes now and look from the place where you are—northward, southward, eastward and westward; for all the land which you see I give to you and your descendants forever. And I will make your descendants as the dust of the earth; so that if a man could number the dust of the earth, then your descendants also could be numbered. Arise, walk in the land through its length and its width, for I give it to you." - - Genesis 13: 14 - 17 (NLT)*

The Lord declared that Abraham's descendants would be a mighty people that could not be counted. He also declared that they would inherit the land of Canaan. Finally, they would be the chosen people of God through whom the Messiah would come into the world.

Wow, what a powerful declaration! However, God had one stipulation that they faithfully serve him.

Jacob

Jacob enjoyed the blessings that came from having declarations being made over his life. He stole his brother's birthright and tricked Isaac into believing he was Esau (Genesis 27). Isaac declared the following over Jacob's life.

> *"From the dew of heaven and the richness of the earth, may God always give you abundant harvests of grain and bountiful new wine. May many nations become your servants, and may they bow down to you. May you be the master over your brothers, and may your mother's sons bow down to you. All who curse you will be cursed, and all who bless you will be blessed." - Gen 27:28-29 (NLT)*

We see these blessings manifesting when he went to live with his uncle Laban. He experiences an increase in his wealth once Jacob began working for him. Genesis 30:27 (NLT) *"Please listen to me," Laban replied. "I have become wealthy, for the Lord has blessed me because of you."*

In Genesis 30: 25-43 (NLT), Jacob is ready to leave his uncle and return home. However, he needs to secure his wealth to support his family. Through his cunning, *"Jacob became very wealthy, with large flocks of sheep and goats, female and male servants, and many camels and donkeys."*

The tradition of making declarations over one's children is passed on by Jacob to his sons and grandsons. His offspring are named for the tribes of Israel - Reuben, Simeon, Levi, Judah, Dan, Naphtali, Gad,

Asher, Issachar, Zebulun, Joseph (Manasseh and Ephraim) and Benjamin. Here we will find one of the most fundamental examples of this practice in the bible.

Jacob's declarations are highly prophetic. They depict the future of his generation. The declarations encapsulate their faults, their consequences and judgments, their hopes, dreams, and mammoth destiny. God through Jacob provided a clear portrait of the future of the Israelites.

Let's examine the declarations made over each son in Genesis 49:3-27 (NLT).

Declaration over Reuben

"Reuben, you are my firstborn, my strength, the child of my vigorous youth. You are first in rank and first in power. But you are as unruly as a flood, and you will be first no longer. For you went to bed with my wife; you defiled my marriage couch.

In Genesis 35:22 (NLT), we see that Reuben slept with his father's concubine Bilhah, who is also the mother of his brothers Dan and Naphtali. He committed an immoral and grave sin. As such, the authority, priesthood, and power that is given to the first born, was distributed among his brothers. Many would argue that he should have been disinherited, but that is not God's way. For Reuben, God through Jacob exercised grace.

Jacob referenced Reuben's unruliness, by comparing it to a flood or water. His father noted the instability in his character and because of it pronounced that he would never excel above his brothers. If you analyze the scriptures, you will note that the tribe of Reuben had no significant rulers, judges, kings, or prophets.

Declaration over Simeon and Levi

"Simeon and Levi are two of a kind; their weapons are instruments of violence. May I never join in their meetings; may I never be a party to their plans. For in their anger, they murdered men, and they crippled oxen just for sport. A curse on their anger, for it is fierce; a curse on their wrath, for it is cruel. I will scatter them among the descendants of Jacob; I will disperse them throughout Israel."

Simeon and Levi were the second and third born. They both were equally responsible for the demise of the men of Shechem, who raped their sister Dinah (Genesis 34:25-29). They were cruel men who inflicted hurt rather than forgiveness or mercy. Remember, God forgets nothing. No evil deed goes unpunished and as such, God had Jacob prophesy a harsh declaration over their lives.

They suffered from the hand of the spirit of anger, which comes under the stronghold of jealousy and rooms with the spirit of murder. They were reckless and willful. God could not allow a spirit of anger to proliferate itself throughout His people. If so, Israel would have become a nation more like the Babylonians and Assyrians; seeking to conquer everybody else. Especially as they were destined to be like the sands on the beach. So, Jacob declared that they would be scattered among the children of Israel.

When Moses took the Israelites into the desert, the tribes of Levi and Simeon decreased. Simeon had to share land with Judah, and Levi did not inherit any land for themselves, in the Promised Land. Nonetheless, they redeemed themselves and inherited God rather than land. From Levi came the priesthood, which included Moses and Aaron.

Declaration over Judah

> *"Judah, your brothers will praise you. You will grasp your enemies by the neck. All your relatives will bow before you. Judah, my son, is a young lion that has finished eating its prey. Like a lion he crouches and lies down; like a lioness—who dares to rouse him? The scepter will not depart from Judah, nor the ruler's staff from his descendants, until the coming of the one to whom it belongs, the one whom all nations will honor. He ties his foal to a grapevine, the colt of his donkey to a choice vine. He washes his clothes in wine, his robes in the blood of grapes. His eyes are darker than wine, and his teeth are whiter than milk."*

Judah was not an exemplary character, but he was redeemable, and God extended His grace to him. To the line of Judah was given the leadership aspect of the firstborn's inheritance. The declaration over Judah is one that encourages strength, courage, and vitality in its reference to a young lion.

The mention of a mature lion foretells of Judah's national prominence and kingship. A lion is said to be the king of the jungle. So, from Judah came many kings. Two of the most infamous was King David and King Solomon. From this tribe would the Prince of Peace arrive into the world. It is significant and noteworthy that Jesus is called the Lion of the tribe of Judah in Revelation 5:5 (NLT).

Finally, Judah's blessing also foretells of wealth. Not only material wealth, but spiritual as well. Who else, but the rich, could afford to tie a donkey to a grapevine and let the animal eat its fill? Who else but the rich could wash their clothes in wine?

Declaration over Zebulun

"Zebulun will settle by the seashore and will be a harbor for ships; his borders will extend to Sidon."

The tribe of Zebulun settled by the sea, near the Mediterranean. They were also supportive and faithful to King David's army. They were expert in war, with all weapons of war. At one time, 50,000 soldiers were from this tribe. In later years, when Jesus Christ begun His ministry, they were one of the first to hear him preach in Galilee.

Declaration over Issachar

"Issachar is a sturdy donkey, resting between two saddle packs. When he sees how good the countryside is and how pleasant the land, he will bend his shoulder to the load and submit himself to hard labor."

The prophecy over Issachar seems lovely at first glance; however, the final words indicate that these people would eventually find themselves in slavery. Their numbers were the third largest of the Israelites at one time, and this attracted the attention and ire of their enemies, who often sought to enslave them. They were conquered by the Assyrians and exiled.

Declaration over Dan

"Dan will govern his people, like any other tribe in Israel. Dan will be a snake beside the road, a poisonous viper along the path that bites the horse's hooves so its rider is thrown off. I trust in you for salvation, O Lord!"

There are many parts, to the declaration made over the life of Dan. All came through. From Dan came Samson, who was one of the most popular judges of his time. He was strong, brave, and fierce. The declaration made over Dan shows him to be a danger, which was hidden. They were the cause of Israel's judgment in many instances. Ultimately, Dan brought and sustained idolatry in Israel.

They had a legacy of man-made idol worship. Nonetheless, there is redemption for them. The final part of the prophecy shows us that Jesus Christ will redeem this tribe.

Declaration over Gad

"Gad will be attacked by marauding bands, but he will attack them when they retreat."

The men of Gad were valiant and fair men. Even though, when they reached the promised land, they were among the first to receive their portion, Gad did not possess it, until all Israelites had conquered their enemies. Just like the tribe of Zebulun, the men of Gad were soldiers in David's army. However, they also suffered frequent oppression by other armies (Jeremiah 49:1). They too were eventually exiled.

Declaration over Asher

"Asher will dine on rich foods and produce food fit for kings."

The prophecy made for Asher was most favorable. They lived in a land that provided for their needs and they were oft blessed with luxury. But Asher was tested many times to prove their faithfulness to both Israel and God Almighty, in some instances they failed. They did not drive out the Canaanites and they often did not join the battles of the other Israelites, for fear of offending the people they traded with.

Declaration over Naphtali

"Naphtali is a doe set free that bears beautiful fawns."

At the time when Jesus, the Messiah walked the earth, he spent a lot of time in *"the land of Zebulun and the land of Naphtali, by the way of the sea, beyond the Jordan, Galilee of the Gentiles: The people who sat in darkness have seen a great light, and upon those who sat in the region and shadow of death light has dawned"* (Matthew 4:12-16)

Declaration over Joseph

"Joseph is the foal of a wild donkey, the foal of a wild donkey at a spring— one of the wild donkeys on the ridge. Archers attacked him savagely; they shot at him and harassed him. But his bow remained taut, and his arms were strengthened by the hands of the Mighty One of Jacob, by the Shepherd, the Rock of Israel. May the God of your father help you; may the Almighty bless you with the blessings of the heavens above, and blessings of the watery depths below, and blessings of the breasts and womb. May my fatherly blessings on you surpass the blessings of my ancestors, reaching to the heights of the eternal hills. May these blessings rest on the head of Joseph, who is a prince among his brothers."

A tribe was not named after Joseph, but after his two sons Manasseh and Ephraim. They received a great blessing from Jacob in Genesis 48. This we will also review later. But the declaration made over Joseph's life was a proclamation of what his life was like and a prophecy of what blessings his generation would enjoy.

His brothers tried to overcome him, but they could not prevail against him, because Jehovah God strengthened him. Anywhere he went, his masters were blessed. He was fruitful, abounding wherever he was planted. He was made second in command to Pharaoh. He led the people of Egypt through seven years of famine.

Declaration over Benjamin

"Benjamin is a ravenous wolf, devouring his enemies in the morning and dividing his plunder in the evening."

Benjamin was a cruel and fierce tribe. This tribe gave us the two Saul's from the bible. The latter, apostle Paul, was formerly known as Saul. He eventually became a Christian and was known as the Apostle of Grace. However, before he met Jesus Christ and was blinded, he persecuted the early Christians. He persecuted, killed, and threw many people into prison.

In Acts 8:1-3 (NLT), shows us that "Saul was one of the witnesses, and he agreed completely with the killing of Stephen." From them also came King Saul. 1 Samuel 14:47-52 (NLT) *"Now when Saul had secured his grasp on Israel's throne, he fought against his enemies in every direction—against Moab, Ammon, Edom, the kings of Zobah, and the Philistines. And wherever he turned, he was victorious. He performed great deeds and conquered the Amalekites, saving Israel from all those who had plundered them."*

From them also came Ehud (Judges 3:15-23, NLT), who killed a Moabite King, Eglon. He used a double-edged dagger that was about a foot long. This King oppressed Israel for tributes. Ehud then led the Israelite men into battle. Judges 3: 29-30 (NLT), *"They attacked the Moabites and killed about 10,000 of their strongest and most able-bodied warriors. Not one of them escaped. So, Moab was conquered by Israel that day, and there was peace in the land for eighty years.*

Judges 19 and 20, encapsulates the nature of Benjamin. It tells the tale of men wanting to sodomize a Levite but raped and killed his concubine instead. This led to a war against the tribe of Benjamin in

Gibeah. Their 26,700 warriors were too much for the other tribes. They initially slaughtered 22,000 men, then 18,000 men. But on the third day, God gave them up to Israel and 25,000 died.

The 600 who escaped were later found and killed. Judges 20:46-48 (NLT) *"So that day the tribe of Benjamin lost 25,000 strong warriors armed with swords, leaving only 600 men who escaped to the rock of Rimmon, where they lived for four months. And the Israelites returned and slaughtered every living thing in all the towns—the people, the livestock, and everything they found. They also burned down all the towns they came to."*

God does not tolerate immorality, perversion, and homosexuality among his people. The tribe of Benjamin suffered a fate like that of Sodom and Gomorrah, who were the descendants of Ham. We explored their story earlier. Also noteworthy is Mordecai and Esther, who were also from the tribe of Benjamin. God strategically placed them in the Persian King's palace. Esther's beauty beguiled the King and he loved her dearly.

Esther 2:17 (ESV) *"the king loved Esther more than all the women, and she won grace and favor in his sight more than all the virgins, so that he set the royal crown on her head and made her queen instead of Vashti."*

Haman developed a hatred for Mordecai and plotted to massacre the people of Israel. His plans were thwarted. Esther fasted and sought God for the King's favor so that she could intercede for Israel. Esther feasted with the King for several days and when the time came, told him of her distress and Haman's plot. Mordecai was exalted by the king and Haman was hung on the same gallows, which he prepared for Mordecai.

Declaration over Ephraim and Manasseh

"May the God before whom my grandfather Abraham and my father, Isaac, walked - the God who has been my shepherd

all my life, to this very day, the Angel who has redeemed me from all harm may he bless these boys. May they preserve my name and the names of Abraham and Isaac. And may their descendants multiply greatly throughout the earth." - Genesis 48:16 (NLT)

"...Manasseh will also become a great people, but his younger brother will become even greater. And his descendants will become a multitude of nations. ...The people of Israel will use your names when they give a blessing. They will say, 'May God make you as prosperous as Ephraim and Manasseh.' In this way, Jacob put Ephraim ahead of Manasseh." - Genesis 48:19-20 (NLT)

Joseph received two portions of blessings for himself and through Ephraim and Manasseh. Some would even say he received three times the blessings as his brothers. His father, Jacob, adopted Joseph's boys as his own. As such, they share in Jacob's inheritance equally with Jacob's own sons.

Even though Joseph placed Manasseh at the right hand of his father, Jacob switched hands. Do you remember that the right hand is seen as a more favorable position? It is a position of pre-eminence. In Mark 14:62 (NLT), it states that Jesus Christ is seated at the right hand of the Father. So, the higher blessing was for the youngest son. Ephraim received a double portion of the blessings pronounced on him and his brother.

Even in recent times, the Jews still pronounce the blessing "May God make you as Ephraim and Manasseh" on their children, as Jacob proclaimed they would. You should too. This blessing has many layers, which are not apparent at first. It carries a declaration about the character, status, well-being, future generation, and children of whomever are blessed. It is a simple but comprehensive declaration.

It is important to note that Jacob, whose name was changed to Israel after he wrestled an angel of God, first blessed the sons of Joseph. Ephraim, who was the youngest and Manasseh. They received the first portion, as shown in Genesis 48 (NLT). Then, Jacob made declarations over his first wife, Leah's sons (Reuben, Simeon, Levi, Judah, Issachar, and Zebulun). His other sons were blessed afterwards.

Moses

The gatekeeper of God's law also made many declarations over the children of Israel. Before Moses died, he reinforced the blessings spoken to the children of Israel, in the desert, on Mount Nebo in Moab. The Blessings of Moses are found in Deuteronomy 33 (NLT).

This is the blessing that Moses, the man of God, gave to the people of Israel before his death:

"The Lord came from Mount Sinai and dawned upon us from Mount Seir; he shone forth from Mount Paran and came from Meribah-kadesh with flaming fire at his right hand. Indeed, he loves his people; all his holy ones are in his hands. They follow in his steps and accept his teaching. Moses gave us the Lord's instruction, the special possession of the people of Israel. The Lord became king in Israel when the leaders of the people assembled, when the tribes of Israel gathered as one."

Moses said this about the tribe of Reuben: *"Let the tribe of Reuben live and not die out, though they are few in number."*

Moses said this about the tribe of Judah: *"O Lord, hear the cry of Judah and bring them together as a people. Give them strength to defend their cause; help them against their enemies!"*

Moses said this about the tribe of Levi: *"O Lord, you have given your Thummim and Urim—the sacred lots—to your faithful servants the Levites. You put them to the test at Massah and struggled with them at the waters of Meribah. The Levites obeyed your word and guarded your covenant. They were more loyal to you than to their own parents. They ignored their relatives and did not acknowledge their own children. They teach your regulations to Jacob; they give your instructions to Israel. They present incense before you and offer whole burnt offerings on the altar. Bless the ministry of the Levites, O Lord, and accept all the work of their hands. Hit their enemies where it hurts the most; strike down their foes so they never rise again."*

Moses said this about the tribe of Benjamin: *"The people of Benjamin are loved by the Lord and live in safety beside him. He surrounds them continuously and preserves them from every harm."*

Moses said this about the tribes of Joseph: *"May their land be blessed by the Lord with the precious gift of dew from the heavens and water from beneath the earth; with the rich fruit that grows in the sun, and the rich harvest produced each month; with the finest crops of the ancient mountains, and the abundance from the everlasting hills; with the best gifts of the earth and its bounty, and the favor of the one who appeared in the burning bush. May these blessings rest on Joseph's head, crowning the brow of the prince among his brothers. Joseph has the majesty of a young bull; he has the horns of a wild ox. He will gore distant nations, even to the ends of the earth.*

This is my blessing for the multitudes of Ephraim and the thousands of Manasseh."

Moses said this about the tribes of Zebulun and Issachar: *"May the people of Zebulun prosper in their travels. May the people of Issachar prosper at home in their tents. They summon the people to the mountain to offer proper sacrifices there. They benefit from the riches of the sea and the hidden treasures in the sand."*

Moses said this about the tribe of Gad: *"Blessed is the one who enlarges Gad's territory! Gad is poised there like a lion to tear off an arm or a head. The people of Gad took the best land for themselves; a leader's share was assigned to them. When the leaders of the people were assembled, they carried out the Lord's justice and obeyed his regulations for Israel."*

Moses said this about the tribe of Dan: *"Dan is a lion's cub, leaping out from Bashan."*

Moses said this about the tribe of Naphtali: *"O Naphtali, you are rich in favor and full of the Lord's blessings; may you possess the west and the south."*

Moses said this about the tribe of Asher: *"May Asher be blessed above other sons; may he be esteemed by his brothers; may he bathe his feet in olive oil. May the bolts of your gates be of iron and bronze; may you be secure all your days."*

"There is no one like the God of Israel. He rides across the heavens to help you, across the skies in majestic splendor. The eternal God is your refuge, and his everlasting arms are under you. He drives out the enemy before you; he cries out, 'Destroy them!'

So, Israel will live in safety, prosperous Jacob in security, in a land of grain and new wine, while the heavens drop down dew. How blessed you are, O Israel! Who else is like you, a people saved by the Lord? He is your protecting shield and your triumphant sword! Your enemies will cringe before you, and you will stomp on their backs!"

David

It is oft said that David is a man after God's own heart and that is true. David was flawed, but he always sought God with a broken and contrite heart. He never disowned the blame and he repented continually for his sin. David was a shepherd. This not only shows him as a leader of many, but also a caregiver.

David wrote the book of Psalms. Only one who has spent immense time in the presence of God could produce such beautiful, eloquent, and praiseworthy messages and adorations for God. David was special to God. Not just because he was King, but because he sought a genuine relationship with Abba Father.

For his devotion, God enacted a covenant with David, just as he did Abraham. Today it is referred to as the 'Davidic covenant.' This covenant was a proclamation by God, for the house or children of David, of whom, Christ, the Messiah would come. There was only one stipulation, that they continually be obedient to God.

The declaration was also different in that, it was God who made a promise to David. One must understand that Yahweh, is the King of Kings, all His promises are declarations and decrees. They cannot be eroded by anyone or time. They are everlasting.

The promise shown here, is taken from 2 Samuel 7:8-17 (NLT).

"Now go and say to my servant David, 'This is what the Lord of Heaven's Armies has declared: I took you from tending sheep in the pasture and selected you to be the leader of my people Israel. I have been with you wherever you have gone, and I

have destroyed all your enemies before your eyes. Now I will make your name as famous as anyone who has ever lived on the earth! And I will provide a homeland for my people Israel, planting them in a secure place where they will never be disturbed. Evil nations won't oppress them as they've done in the past, starting from the time I appointed judges to rule my people, Israel. And I will give you rest from all your enemies.

"'Furthermore, the Lord declares that he will make a house for you—a dynasty of kings! For when you die and are buried with your ancestors, I will raise up one of your descendants, your own offspring, and I will make his kingdom strong. He is the one who will build a house—a temple—for my name. And I will secure his royal throne forever. I will be his father, and he will be my son. If he sins, I will correct and discipline him with the rod, like any father would do. But my favor will not be taken from him, as I took it from Saul, whom I removed from your sight. Your house and your kingdom will continue before me for all time, and your throne will be secure forever.'"

So, Nathan went back to David and told him everything the Lord had said in this vision.

This promise comprises several things: Israel would have a place of their own. There would be no more misery from other nations. God would establish an everlasting Davidic kingdom, Davidic house, and a Davidic throne. He would provide fatherly care for all of David's offspring. This was the sealed covenant that David received from Yahweh, for his children.

As you have read, we begin and end, with God. He is the alpha and omega. The beginning and the end. God is the author of all the declarations, made by these men, for their children. Likewise, allow

God to fill your mouth with purpose-filled and appropriate blessings for your children.

Seek His wisdom and walk in understanding of His divine will.

Declarations For My Life

Introduction

Before we start with the declarations for our sons and daughters, it is imperative that we break off the curses over our own lives and renounce every sin. The beginning of the end, the key to breaking off the old shackles and setting a proper foundation for our children, starts with us. So, as we proceed, we will tackle denouncing all sin, generational curses, witchcraft curses, taking back all rights and privileges, which we have given to the enemy. And we will cancel every curse, known and unknown that has either been spoken over us, or sent against our family and us.

There are several steps to this process. You will be required to:

1. Yield to God
2. Confront sin
3. Acknowledge Jesus Christ as Lord and Savior
4. Take back rights and privileges
5. Cancel curses (known and unknown)
6. Cancel the assignment of the enemy
7. Go on the offensive
8. Maintain the edge of protection

Yielding To God

What's required can be summed up in one word, surrender. You **MUST** surrender to Jehovah. It is not an option. It is a requirement. There is no way that you will have a chance against the forces of hell unless you give over to the sovereign power and authority of God. You must let His will be done in your life and lay yours down.

Demonic spirits can easily spot a fake from the real thing. They can tell if you are a sold-out Christian who is living a life completely led by God. Being anything else will leave you open to intense spiritual attack and even demonic possession if you are not careful. In spiritual warfare, the battle belongs to the Lord. There is no real power that you have of yourself.

All your arsenal and weapons, power and authority come from the Mighty One, the Commander of the hosts of heaven. Therefore, you must submit fully to Him. You can't fool any spirit, good or bad, which operates in the spiritual realm. To them your true nature is always on display.

So, be prepared to hand over every facet of your life to God. This includes the physical, spiritual, social, psychological, emotional, financial and anything else that is a part of your existence.

Once you give over to Jehovah, you have access to a limitless God. One who is forever sovereign. One who is all powerful, all knowing and is without blemish or stain. He has none of your weaknesses and his strength extends beyond human comprehension. The Rock of Ages will fight every one of your battles, and you can rest in the assurance that He has already won the war.

When you yield to Him, and He takes over your life there are many benefits that you will see manifest.

You will have access to:

1. An ever-present Father
2. An unwavering Friend
3. Unconditional and persistent love
4. Grace and mercy
5. Divine wisdom, knowledge and understanding
6. Divine favor
7. Provision for your every need
8. Comfort in times of distress
9. Peace in times of upheaval
10. Knowledge of your true purpose and destiny
11. Angels that encampeth round about you
12. Guardian angels that guide you
13. The unlimited resources of God and heaven

And so much more!

The bible says:

> *"Now therefore, fear the Lord, serve Him in sincerity and in truth, ... Serve the Lord! And if it seems evil to you to serve the Lord, choose for yourselves this day whom you will serve ..." – Joshua 24:14-15 (NKJV)*

There were times the children of Israel had to declare openly that Jehovah was their God. This was necessary so that there could be a witness and the witnesses were themselves, as indicated further in Joshua 24:22. But also, their words were a declaration to everyone, who their God was and that they had committed to serve him only.

You too will have to make this kind of declaration.

Further in Matthew 6:24, we receive clarification as to why we need to yield to God.

> *"No one can serve two masters; for either he will hate the one and love the other, or else he will be loyal to the one and despise the other. You cannot serve God and mammon." - Matthew 6:24 (NKJV)*

For some of you, this commitment might be difficult because you will go against everything that you once knew. And you will go against the beliefs and guidance of your own family and friends. However, rest assured Jesus addressed this issue Mathew 10:34. So, regardless of those who stand against you, or threaten to abandon you, you can have no part of God unless you forsake all others.

> *"Do not think that I came to bring peace on earth. I did not come to bring peace but a sword. For I have come to 'set a man against his father, a daughter against her mother, and a daughter-in-law against her mother-in-law;' and 'a man's enemies will be those of his own household.' He who loves father or mother more than Me is not worthy of Me. And he who loves son or daughter more than Me is not worthy of Me. And he who does not take his cross and follow Me is not worthy of Me. He who finds his life will lose it, and he who loses his life for My sake will find it." - Mathew 10:34-39 (NKJV)*

It might not be an easy decision, but it is one that is worthwhile. If Jesus Christ can make the ultimate sacrifice to die for your sins on Calvary's cross after being scourged and whipped to an inch of His life. After being ridiculed, spat on, betrayed and chastised – can you not offer up your fidelity to Him?

If the answer is yes, then continue reading to submit yourself to Yahweh and let His perfect will operate in your life. "... whoever of you does not forsake all that he has cannot be My disciple." - Luke 14:33 (NKJV).

Prayer

Lord, I submit my mind, my body, my spirit, my soul, and everything that I am to the will of the Holy Spirit.

I give over my will freely to you Heavenly Father, for the accomplishment of your purpose and so that your will can be done in the Earth.

I bow to You oh Great Eternal King and Lord and I humbly come into Your presence.

Everything that I am or ever hope to be is in You, Powerful One.

Lord, you are the Faithful God whom I will serve forever. I pledge to obey Your perfect will. I pledge to yield to Your call. Help me to be obedient and allow Your will to work in my life and the life of my family and children.

Come now Lord, let thy will be done and Your power and Your glory reign forever more.

In the mighty name Jesus, I pray, amen.

Congratulations, you have taken the first step. The Lord will now move you strategically. He will guide you into your purpose and destiny. He will train you up for your assignments and all that you will do for Him. And most of all, Ye will be faithful to you and your family.

You must now be attentive and listen out for Him to direct you in your daily life. With your friends, family and even your coworkers or man on the street, God might ask you to do things that you won't expect and some things, which might make you uncomfortable. But remember, you have yielded your life and will over to Him. So, be attentive, yield, heed his commands and do what He requires of you.

For some of you, this might not be tomorrow or even next month. For others, you might feel His prodding in the next few moments. He might start asking you to address areas of sin in your life. Just be open to following His direction and feel free to ask Him for clear guidance and direction. He will answer your requests.

And even still, there are those of you who will now start to remember those things, which God requested of you in the past. Now, you can freely operate from a place of obedience, knowing that Jehovah Shalom will guide you through it. No matter how arduous the task may seem. There is nothing too big for our God.

"Therefore, you shall be careful to do as the Lord your God has commanded you; you shall not turn aside to the right hand or to the left." - Deuteronomy 5:32 (NKJV)

Repeat the prayer as often as you need to. I pray these prayers almost every day because I constantly wrestle with what my flesh wants to do and what the Lord wants for my life. I find it also helpful to ask God to command my mornings, or to command my day. Repeating these declarations and prayers often will help you to remain faithful to your pledge to God.

Confronting Sin

This is a twofold process. It involves confessing your sins and renouncing your sins. Trust that this might make you uncomfortable, but it is a necessary part of your deliverance.

Confessing Your Sins

Imagine that you are in a courtroom. The judge asks whether you plead guilty or not. Your answer would be you confessing your sins – you are guilty. If you can't openly acknowledge your wrongdoings to the King of Heaven, who is also your judge, then you nor your children will be delivered.

The declarations will be ineffective, and the enemy will build even more strongholds in your life. Your territory will become their territory and you won't have the power to evict them from your lands or your life. You will be ineffective against their attack because you are too stubborn or filled with pride to yield to God and openly confess your sins to him. This then leads to you having no hope, no help and forced to continuously deal with the bombardments of the enemy against you and your family, until someone at some point decides to give over to God.

Have you ever noticed that children usually have the same issues as their parents? Take for example, an alcoholic father, begets alcoholic children. So, if you struggle with drug abuse, alcohol abuse, pornography, perversion and any other grave sin, your children will struggle to defeat the same demons.

But let's get a bit more strategic. The key to being effective in spiritual warfare is to understand that every sin is a demonic presence or stronghold in your life.

Lying, stealing, adultery, fornication, perversion, lust, homosexuality, hate, envy, murder, gluttony, malice, covetousness, possessiveness, disobedience, addiction, laziness, gambling, greed, drunkenness, rebellion, pride, unforgiveness, discord, debauchery, immorality, masturbation, unbelief, gossip, slander, bitterness, insanity, infirmity, hypocrisy, treachery, cruelty, revenge, plundering, backbiting, complaining, heresy, lewdness, profanity, pride, mind control, fear, occultism, idolatry, divination, witchcraft and so many other sins. These demonic manifestations are obstacles the devil uses to get between you and God. And even more so, it is how he forms ties and curses, which later plague your children.

Renouncing Your Sins

It is not enough to simply confess your transgressions. You must turn your back on these sins and deny them. This will help to mitigate their power and influence over your life. You see, we are all sinners and will face temptation daily. No one is perfect, so at times we fall. We yield to temptation and commit sin. However, because we have an advocate in Christ, we can turn to Jesus and confess our sins. He will make petition on our behalf to God the Father if we are sincerely repentant.

It will take willpower and true grit. So, take some time to commit fully to this process. Think about what it will require of you and make the decision to follow through with your decision.

It will take repeated and daily commitment. Drug addiction, alcohol addiction or pornography are not the only sins that have a death grip on some of us and refuses to back away. There are many of us battling with other sins that are equally as strong as pornography, drugs, and alcohol.

For example, in the 21st century, millions of people fall prey to cell phone and social media addiction without even being fully aware. Not to mention the hunger and thirst for instant gratification, likes and recognition. The insatiable appetite for us to go viral and become social media stars. We even use our kids to gain this recognition and put our most personal business on display.

Narcissism is on the rise and selfies are the new cocaine. Technological gadgets are glued to our hands. Our eyes are glued to screens and we have become an anti-social and virtually addicted people. You can't go anywhere and not see this epidemic, glaring at you. That is, if you dare to look away from your screen.

Worse of all, our children are programmed for the same lifestyle from they are babes. They are left with screens to parent them. It is a dangerous and tsunami like trend that is taking over the world. But, if you want to be set free from their power, all you must do is confess them, renounce them, and submit your life to the power of Jesus Christ.

He is stronger than all these low-level demons, powers, principalities, spiritual wickedness, and rulers of darkness that seek to enslave and ultimately kill you. When you renounce your sin, the enemy has no power over you.

He will try to lure you back with the same old sins. But, if you remain under the shadow of the Almighty and resist the enemy, the devil will flee from you. *"Therefore, submit to God. Resist the devil and he will flee from you."- James 4:7 (NKJV).*

Prayer

Lord, I am guilty. I have sinned and come short of the glory of God. I am not worthy of your mercy. But thank God, for the sacrifice and shed blood of Jesus Christ who has redeemed my sins.

Prayer 2

Jehovah, I confess my sins, my transgressions. I have (...list your sins ...).

I am deeply sorry.

Lord, I confess and renounce every sin in my life. I declare myself free from the guile and lure of the enemy.

The devil has no power over me, and I am redeemed by the blood of Christ.

I renounce any affiliation with demons, powers, principalities, rulers of darkness, and spiritual wickedness in high places.

I renounce any affiliation with witches, warlocks, incubus and succubus spirits, freemasonry, enchantments, obeah men, obeah women, voodoo priest and priestesses and any other agent, satanist or high priest of the devil and his kingdom.

I renounce, reject, and revoke any evil contract that I or my parents and their forefathers have made with the evil one. No pact with the kingdom of darkness shall stand. None will be supported by my generation, my children or me. Every contract with the enemy is declared canceled, whether they involved me, my parents, my fore parents, my children that are made with the evil one.

I am washed by the blood of Jesus Christ. I am purged by the fire of the Holy Spirit, and I am fed by the Word of God.

I am sold out to Christ, bought with the blood of Jesus Christ and I am free.

In Jesus name, amen.

Acknowledging Jesus Christ as Lord and Savior

Jesus is the way, the truth, and the light. No one comes to the Father but through Him.

And Jesus, when he was baptized, went up straightway out of the water: and, lo, the heavens were opened unto him, and he saw the Spirit of God descending like a dove, and lighting upon him: And lo a voice from heaven, saying, this is my beloved Son, in whom I am well pleased. - Matthew 3:16-17

"The time is here, and the kingdom of God is at hand. Repent, and believe in the gospel." - Mark 1:15

Jesus Christ died for our sins according to the Scriptures, that He was buried, and then He was resurrected on the third day. – 1 Cor. 15:1-4 (NKJV

Romans 4:25 and 5:2 tells us that He was delivered over to death for our sins and then was raised to life to put us right with God. By faith in this, then, we have peace with God through our Lord Jesus Christ, through whom we have gained access by faith into this grace in which we now stand.

If You confess with Your mouth, "Jesus is Lord," and believe in Your heart that God raised Him from the dead, you will be saved. For with Your heart, you believe and are put right with

God, and it is with Your mouth that You confess and are saved. As the Scripture says, "Anyone who trusts in Him will never be put to shame." - Romans 10:9-11(NKJV)

1 John 1:3-4 says that which we have seen and heard we declare to You, that You also may have fellowship with us; and truly our fellowship is with the Father and with His Son Jesus Christ. We write these things to You that Your joy may be full.

Prayer of Salvation

"Father, I know that I have broken Your laws and my sins have separated me from You. I am terribly sorry, and now I want to turn away from my past sinful life toward You.

Please forgive me and help me avoid sinning again. I believe that Your son, Jesus Christ died for my sins, was resurrected from the dead, is alive and hears my prayer.

I invite Jesus to become the Lord of my life, to rule and reign in my heart from this day forward.

Please send Your Holy Spirit to help me obey You, and to do Your will for the rest of my life.

In Jesus' name I pray, Amen.

Prayer 2

I acknowledge Jesus Christ as my Lord and Savior. He was crucified and died on the cross for my sins. He rose again from the grave having defeated death, hell, and the grave.

I am redeemed, bought with a price. Jesus paid for my sins and now I am washed clean by his blood. Old sins are passed away, behold all things have been made new.

My life, my heart, my desires – everything that I am, I am sold out to God, and I am His.

Jesus Christ is Lord of all.

Once you accept Jesus Christ as your Lord and Savior, you will also bring over the blessings of Abraham into your life. You and your children after you will have access to those promises and you will bring the glory of God into your family.

Taking Back Rights and Privileges

We all invite people - friends and family - into our homes. At first, they are mindful and usually make requests when they want something to eat, to drink, or even a place to sit. However, after a few visits, they seem to make themselves at home.

After a while, they come over uninvited, and some might even have a key to your place. They readily go to your fridge to take what they want. And there are those who even have the free rein to spend the night and even stay over while we are not there. They now have certain rights and privileges, which you have permitted for them to have.

It is the same with demonic spirits. We have consciously or subconsciously provided an open door, window, or gateway into our lives – through sin – that they gain position of legal access to us. When the devil goes to God, to petition Jehovah on His throne he presents his case. And God hears every case in heaven.

We see this, especially in Job.

Now there was a day when the sons of God came to present themselves before the Lord, and Satan also came among them. And the Lord said to Satan, "From where do you come?"

So, Satan answered the Lord and said, "From going to and fro on the earth, and from walking back and forth on it."

Then the Lord said to Satan, "Have you considered My servant Job, that there is none like him on the earth, a blameless and upright man, one who fears God and shuns evil?"

So, Satan answered the Lord and said, "Does Job fear God for nothing? Have You not made a hedge around him, around his household, and around all that he has on every side? You have blessed the work of his hands, and his possessions have increased in the land. But now, stretch out Your hand and touch all that he has, and he will surely curse You to Your face!"

And the Lord said to Satan, "Behold, all that he has is in your power; only do not lay a hand on his person."

So, Satan went out from the presence of the Lord. – Job 1:6-12 (NKJV)

Now, the devil petitioned God to get access to Job, because he could not do so otherwise. Job was always making atonement to God for the sins of his family – early in the morning. Imagine, how it must be for the rest of us who are not so vigilant and faithful to God.

They constantly accuse us to God and if we fall prey to their temptations, then we give them access not only to us, but possible and eventually to our sons and daughters. This is where generational curses begin. Remember in warfare, there are rules of engagement – even in the spiritual realm. And no matter if you are a saint or sinner, the same rules apply to you and your life.

Thankfully, the children of God have a hedge of protection. This is what the devil referred to in Job 1:9 "Have You not made a hedge around him, around his household, and around all that he has on every side?" However, this can be bypassed or removed either by our own indulgence in sin or by the devil making petition to God.

So, to nullify and revoke any access the enemy may have, we must dig up the root! We must take back all rights and privileges. We have already gone through the first couple of steps. However, you must stay away from willfully committing sin against your body, or against God.

That means not committing transgressions such as:

1. Idolatry
2. Murder or heinous criminal acts
3. Sexual immorality
4. Physical or verbal abuse of others
5. Becoming addicted to drugs, alcohol, pornography, social media etc.
6. Having an abortion
7. Participating in the occult, witchcraft, or satanic worship

These are just a few of the more common sins. However, knowingly, and willfully committing sin without confessing and renouncing your transgressions will easily give these demonic entities free rein over your life, your person, and your family.

This revocation of legal rights and deliverance for you, starts with verbal commands. You must command each demon – calling them by name – to go.

Prayer

In the name of Jesus Christ of Nazareth, I stand in the authority and power, which He has given me, and I bind the strongman. I command every spirit of—(name of the sin)—to come out of me and go to a hot dry place touching nothing and no one. Do not return and do no harm to me, my body, or my family. Come out of me now.

(Repeat this portion above, for every area of transgression.)

I command you demon of fornication, lust, sexual immorality, and perversion to come out of me and go to a hot dry place touching nothing and no one. Do not return and do no harm to me, my body, or my family. Come out of me now. And if you return, may you be scourged and consumed by the fire of the Holy Spirit in Jesus name amen.

I take back every legal right and disallow any diabolical mandate, injunction or subverting strategies over my life, my family, or my person.

I nullify the previous rulings and access granted to demons to my life and I take back control. I establish divine borders and hedges patrolled by the angels of the Lord. And I establish the precepts of Jehovah in my territory.

I tear down the high places and I decree and declare that every stronghold of the enemy is destroyed. It is annihilated. It is grounded to dust and no other stronghold shall be erected in its place.

Mighty God of Daniel, war on my behalf. Reinforce my borders. Secure my hedges, my walls, my doors, and my windows. Challenge my enemies, scatter them with confusion in their meetings and let them have no victory over my life, in Jesus name.

I thank you for your grace and mercy. I thank you for the blood of Jesus Christ. I thank you for the victory in battle. I thank you for divine favor. Release your Holy Spirit to occupy, guide and oversee my life, my family and territory.

I yield to Your will in my life.

May Your heavenly seal be on all that I have and possess in this life, in Jesus name amen.

Maintaining the Edge of Protection

Sometimes we become forgetful, ungrateful, and lackadaisical. We forget that our lives are about spiritual warfare, and that the enemy never gives up. He simply waits until we have grown either tired or forgetful. When we drop our guard, he moves in and rebuilds. As such, we must be vigilant. We must maintain our edge of protection. Keep praying and making godly declarations over your life and family.

Declarations for My Sons

Isaiah 44:3-4 (NKJV)

...I will pour My Spirit on your descendants, and My blessing on your offspring; They will spring up among the grass like willows by the watercourses.

I declare and decree that the hand of God will forever be on my sons' lives.

I declare and decree that my sons are blessed. In them are found the innocence of Jehovah. They shall serve him faithfully.

My sons shall not tarry in the council or the dwelling of the ungodly. They shall be standard bearers of the Kingdom of God.

My sons will walk in obedience, humility, faith, wisdom, understanding, strength, compassion, and respect from conception.

My sons will always bring great honor to their parents.

The gift of the Holy Spirit will abide in my lineage forever.

I decree that my sons shall speak the tongues of angels and languages of heaven. Demons will fall at their command.

My sons will release people from their prisons. They will be an arrow pointing to God all their days.

I decree that they shall be keepers of the faith. Patient, kind, forgiving, caring, and respectful, to their wives.

I declare and decree in earth and in the heavens that my sons shall burn down the dwellings of their spiritual enemies and in their lives will be truth everlasting.

None of my sons shall leave from under the shadow of the almighty. They will be used of God to shelter the persecuted.

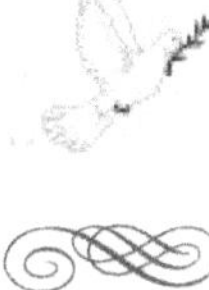

My sons shall bear mighty sons. They will be the Jobs, Daniels, and Josephs of their time.

People will travel to seek their counsel. I declare that they govern the land with fairness and righteousness.

In Jesus name, amen.

Declarations over Their Childhood

May the God before whom my forefather Abraham and Isaac, walked - the God who has been my shepherd all my life, to this very day, the Angel who has redeemed me from all harm may he bless my sons. May they preserve my name and the names of Abraham and Isaac. And may their descendants multiply greatly throughout the earth.

I decree that my sons will live and not die.

I declare and decree that my sons shall be born safely, and, on their arrival, they shall usher in immense joy into everyone's lives.

My sons shall never be abandoned by their fathers. They shall know the stability, and security of a father's love.

They shall grow up rooted in the spiritual and moral values of their parents. My sons shall be hidden in the scriptural reference, to train up a child in the way he should grow, and he will never depart from it.

I declare and decree that the Word of Almighty God shall be a foundation and a night song to my sons in their youth.

I declare and decree that my sons shall never be oppressed, suppressed, or distressed by the hands or taunts of the bully and evil men. They shall be strong fences that prevent the forces of the enemy from plaguing their lands in Jesus name.

Isaiah 49:25 (NKJV)

But thus says the Lord: "Even the captives of the mighty shall be taken away, and the prey of the terrible be delivered; for I will contend with him who contends with you, and I will save your children."

Declarations over Their Education

My mighty sons will be keepers of God's wisdom. They will consume the knowledge of this world like a glass of water. From them will pour mysteries and code breaking information.

I decree and declare that my sons will find favor with their teachers and mentors.

My sons shall excel in all their endeavors. They will be the head and not the tail.

God shall be a close confidant and teacher to my sons. He will keep them under the shadow of the Almighty. Their ways will not be man's ways; but they will be exemplary examples for the kingdom of heaven.

I decree and declare that my sons shall be protected in the classroom and the hallways. The bully will be his friend and my son will lead them to the ways of Almighty God.

The school will be the training ground to ministry for my children. They will be a counsellor to their school mates, even at an early age. They will be endowed with wisdom, knowledge and understanding.

I declare that my sons will be diligent. Always prepared.

I declare and decree that my sons and their sons, even to the twelfth generation will follow the plans that Jesus have for their lives. They will conform to his destined plan for them in deed, action and thought.

My children will rest in the promise that they can do all things through Christ who strengthens them, in Jesus name amen.

DENISE N. FYFFE

Psalm 144:12 (NLT)

May our sons flourish in their youth like well-nurtured plants. May our daughters be like graceful pillars, carved to beautify a palace.

Declarations over Their Work

I decree and declare that my sons will be innovators, leaders, and visionaries.

My sons will be exemplary practitioners of their discipline.

The favor of God shall be with my children. They will set footsteps for others to follow to greatness.

My sons will not be shackled by the office gossip. Nor scorned by the office elite. They will receive good tidings. They will always have favor with all men and women.

My sons will maintain exemplary reputations. They will be bestowed with trust, loyalty and operate in complete honesty with all men.

The office shall also be a place of ministry for my children. They will see the need of people and lead them to Jesus Christ.

The angels of the Lord shall encamp around my children, even in the workplace. They shall guide, guard, and protect them. They shall break down and destroy every workplace stronghold and lead the captives free, in Jesus' name amen.

I John 2:14(NKJV)

I have written to you, young men, because you are strong, and the word of God abides in you, and you have overcome the wicked one.

Declarations over Their Ministry

My sons shall feed the poor. They shall heal the sick. They shall right wrongs and declare the works of the Lord, our God.

I declare and decree that my sons will be oaks and cedars for their pastors, bishops, and leaders.

I declare and decree that the Holy Spirit will stir up the gifts within my sons and they shall operate effectively and obediently unto the God and His will, in Jesus name.

The blood of Jesus shall be a banner over my sons and their sons, and they shall travel to the farthest corners of the world sharing the Gospel of Jesus Christ.

I declare and decree that my sons and their sons even to the twelfth generation shall be missionaries, evangelists, deacons, ministers, pastors, bishops, prophets, and apostles in accordance with the call that God has on their life, in Jesus name.

I declare and decree that prayer shall be a language of intimacy with God for my sons and they shall also wield it in excellence to war successfully against the enemy forces.

I declare and decree that my children shall flow fluidly in the gift of discerning of spirits, word of wisdom, word of knowledge, faith, healing, miracles, prophecy, diverse tongues, and the interpretation of tongues in Jesus name.

Every obstacle set up to stop and destroy my children's ministry shall be destroyed by the fire of Heaven.

Every false gossip, liar, destiny stealer and deceiver sent by Satan to attack my children and their children shall be arrested and charged by the court of Heaven. They shall not succeed in Jesus name.

The blood of Jesus has redeemed my children and they will be faithful to Almighty God all their days, in Jesus name.

May they have favor within the body of Christ always. May they be willing to serve where they are placed and be a beacon to others.

May the light of God shine through their hearts to free those imprisoned by hurt, anger, abuse, jealousy, bitterness, un-forgiveness, generational curses, witchcraft, and every foul thing.

The Word of God shall be a two-edged sword in their mouth. They shall be generals, seasoned in spiritual warfare.

They shall build and grow ministries.

My sons and their sons shall extend the borders of heaven and rally the forces of heaven against the enemies of God.

All their enemies will be cast down, embarrassed, and utterly defeated, in Jesus name amen.

Isaiah 61: 9 (NLT)

Their descendants will be recognized and honored among the nations. Everyone will realize that they are a people the Lord has blessed.

Declarations over Their Marriages

I declare and decree that the wives of my sons and their sons will be beautiful women of God from around the world. Daughters of Abraham.

I declare and decree that my daughters in law, granddaughters in law, even unto the 12th generation shall be rocks of Gibraltar to my sons. At their words, the mountains shall kneel, and the waters shall part. They will be eloquent transcribers of God's word.

I declare that the spirit of separation and divorce shall be without power and influence against my sons and their marriages in Jesus name.

My son's family shall prosper in love, unity, prosperity, loyalty, gentleness, and goodness. They shall forever be one before Almighty God.

My children shall find partners who are their equals in all things.

I decree that my daughters will be evenly yoked with their spouses physically, mentally, emotionally, and spiritually. They will come before God and count him as their Savior, their Lord, and their King.

May Yahweh grant my children the spiritual fortitude to cover their partners in prayer and operate in wisdom.

I decree and declare that my children shall be victorious in spiritual warfare against the enemy for their family, in Jesus name amen.

The blood of Jesus Christ shall protect my children and their children from physical, emotional, and psychological spousal abuse, in Jesus' name amen.

Psalms 112:2 (NKJV)

His descendants will be mighty on earth; The generation of the upright will be blessed.

Declarations over Their Family

I decree that God shall not leave from my son's families, even onto the 12th generation.

I declare and decree that every one of my children and their children shall be saved. They shall accept Jesus as their Lord and Savior and faithfully serve Him in Jesus name.

My children shall love their families and relatives, just as Christ loved the church.

The children of my sons shall honor them for as long as they live.

The wisdom of God shall be granted unto my sons, and they shall nurture and guide their children with divine counsel.

The Holy Spirit shall be a close comfort to my children even in the womb and they will be filled with the Holy Spirit.

The Lord God of Israel shall be a fierce protector of my son's children and fight their battles.

I decree and declare that my sons shall raise up their families in the way of the Lord God of Host and they shall never depart from it, in Jesus name.

Proverbs 2:20 (NLT)

Follow the steps of good men instead, and stay on the paths of the righteous

Declarations over Their Health

I declare and decree that my sons and my sons' sons shall walk in supernatural health from birth. They shall bring happiness to all peoples.

My sons are fearfully and wonderfully made. Their bodies shall function in the manner that God intend.

My sons shall live in perfect health and shall not be oppressed by the stronghold of infirmity.

I declare and decree that every plague that hounds my sons and their sons shall be destroyed by the fire of Almighty God, in Jesus' name.

My sons shall wield the shield of faith and quench every fiery dart of the enemy.

The Lord is the strength of my son's lives.

No sickness or plague shall come nigh the dwelling of my sons, and their sons even to the twelfth generation.

I declare and decree that the fire of God shall burn out any sickness or disease that would operate in my sons and grandsons in the name of Jesus.

Lord God let your virtue touch the lives of my sons and heal them.

The beauty of my sons and grandsons shall be as the olive tree.

The youth of my sons even to the twelfth generation shall be like an eagle's.

I declare and decree that every tumor in the bodies of my sons and their sons shall melt away, in Jesus name.

Almighty God shall bless the bread and water of my sons and take sickness away from them.

No mental, physical, psychological, or emotional illnesses or disease shall overcome and suppress my children. They shall walk with angels and live in bounty and blessings.

I declare and decree that no hereditary spirits of sickness shall prevail over my children, in Jesus name, amen.

Genesis 18:19 (NLT)

I have singled him out so that he will direct his sons and their families to keep the way of the Lord by doing what is right and just. Then I will do for Abraham all that I have promised.

Declarations over Their Wealth

All my sons, their sons, and their sons' sons shall be kingdom financiers. Their wells shall be more bountiful than Jacob's well.

My sons shall not dwell in poverty. They shall conquer this stronghold and bring prosperity to the land, in Jesus name.

I decree and declare that my sons shall live in the prosperity of Kings.

The Lord God Almighty shall release the wealth of the wicked into the hands of my sons.

Abba shall open the flood gates of heaven into the hands of my sons.

I decree and declare that my sons will not incur debt. They shall not be constantly bombarded by debt collectors. My sons shall increase in wealth and spend with wisdom and understanding

My sons shall be the benefactors of scholarships, grants, and bursaries.

My sons shall give, and it shall return unto them good measure, pressed down, shaken together, and running over (Luke 6:38).

The pockets and wallets of my sons shall be divinely sealed. No holes shall be found in them.

The barns of my sons shall be filled with plenty, and their presses burst with new wine (Prov. 3:10).

I declare and decree that my sons will find favor with all people, and they shall put money into their hands, and they shall live in prosperity forever and ever, amen.

I decree and declare that my sons shall never lack wheat, shall never lack honey, shall never lack from the vines, and shall never lack in the fields. My sons shall reap from the most barren of fields and shall return the land to great harvest.

The Lord God Almighty shall anoint the heads of my sons with oil, and let their cup run over, in Jesus name, Amen.

The land of my sons, and their sons and their son's sons shall be blessed. The hills shall be wet with rain and the valleys shall be filled with rivers.

May the archangels of God protect the storehouses of my sons, in Jesus name, Amen.

I declare that every demonic assignment against my children's finances shall be nullified

Failure, poverty, lack and debt shall have no power over my son's finances, in the name of Jesus.

I decree that my sons shall seek ye first the kingdom of God and all His righteous, and all other things shall be added unto them.

The caterpillar, cankerworm, palmerworm, and locust that attack the finances and blessings of my children, shall die by fire. They shall be destroyed by the forces of Heaven.

My sons and their sons shall be blessed in the city, blessed in the fields. Blessed when they come and when they go in Jesus name.

I declare and decree that my God will provide for my children. He is their Jehovah-Jireh.

Every hole that appears in my children's bag shall be closed and they shall all tithe to the King of Kings, in Jesus name amen.

Colossians 2:15 (NKJV)
Having disarmed principalities and powers, He made a public spectacle of them, triumphing over them in it.

Declarations over Their Security

I declare and decree that my sons will never suffer abuse. They will never be misused. Their warring angels will always protect them, in Jesus name.

I declare that the Lord God of Israel will protect their innocence and keep them whole. He will be their father, and king.

I decree and declare that the adversary shall be demolished, scattered and his plans made as dust. He shall never overtake my sons and their children.

The hand of the Almighty One shall forever be a shadow and hiding place for my sons and their family.

I decree and declare that the winds of confusion shall sweep into the house of my sons' enemies.

The enemies' meetings of conspiracy and plot making, against my sons and my sons' sons, shall be cancelled. They shall have no friendly abode.

The fires of the Holy Spirit shall rage in the homes of my sons' enemies, and they shall be scorched and purged, in Jesus name.

I bind and rebuke and cast into the lake of fire, all demonic reinforcements sent against my sons, by Satan to attack their life.

I declare and decree that the Holy Spirit will loose confusion, and let all their enemies attack each other, in the name of Jesus.

I take authority over the princes and powers and rulers of darkness and demons, which rise against my sons and their families, and I cast them back to the pit of hell. Their plans shall come to naught, and their camps shall be made desolate in Jesus name.

I decree and declare that my sons shall sing songs of war and they shall be equipped in spiritual warfare.

My sons shall fight valiantly with the sword and their armor shall never be lacking or neglected. They shall be fluent with the arrows of God, and they shall crush the necks of their enemies, in the name of Jesus Christ.

Let the high places of wickedness be removed from the lives of my sons and their sons' sons.

May the angels of God encampeth round about my sons and deliver them into the hands of Almighty God.

I quench every fiery dart, torch and launch pad of wickedness set against my sons in the name of Jesus.

I decree and declare that my sons shall not be burned by the fires of the enemy.

I bind the lips of the witches, warlocks, gossips, and enchanters, who are sent against my sons. They shall choke on their words and be made dumb, in Jesus name.

I declare and decree that their words, gossip, false witness, incantations, and spells shall be reversed from my sons, in Jesus name.

I decree and declare that all curses of witchcraft, sorcery, and divination over the lives of my sons, shall be broken in the name of Jesus Christ.

Jehovah Rappa shall strengthen and reinforce the bars of the gates, doors, and windows of my sons, in Jesus name.

Oh God of gods and King of kings, let the gates of preaching, teaching, the flow of the Holy Spirit, evangelism, apostolic doctrine, and deliverance; of my sons, and my sons' sons be constantly repaired and mended, in Jesus name.

Execute judgement over the fowler as he rises up against my sons; cripple his hand and feet, blind his eyes, and leave him utterly destroyed, in Jesus name.

Let the thief be broken, let the murderer be broken, let the chief agent be broken, let the kingdom of darkness be broken and utterly scattered in their gathering against my sons.

Jehovah will be unto my sons as a brother. They shall establish and keep his laws. No evil, curse, demon, or false thing shall overtake my sons.

Every curse and demon from hell will be defeated and reversed in their course. My sons and grandsons, even to the 12th generation, shall be protected by the warring angels from heaven; in God will they have eternal favor.

In the mighty name of Jesus Christ, Amen.

Philippians 4:6

Be anxious for nothing, but in everything by prayer and supplication, with thanksgiving, let your requests be made known to God

Conclusion

This book, Declarations for my Sons, rests upon the foundation of the Word of Almighty God. Several scriptures truly reflect the intent and potency of declarations, specifically those entrenched in the word of God.

Hebrews 4:12,16 (KJV) states that:

"For the word of God is quick, and powerful, and sharper than any two-edged sword, piercing even to the dividing asunder of soul and spirit, and of the joints and marrow, and is a discerner of the thoughts and intents of the heart...Let us therefore come boldly unto the throne of grace, that we may obtain mercy, and find grace to help in time of need."

In warfare, your enemy will only respect and fear that which is greater than he. There is no one greater than Jehovah, for He is the great and terrible God, the creator of all things. Hebrews highlights the very nature and purpose of His word. Therefore, it is only logical that the declarations you make is cemented in the word of God. Also, with the word of God, one can boldly approach the throne of grace, where you are assured grace and mercy.

May the God of our fathers and children, grant you many blessings. May your children partake in the Abrahamic and Davidic covenants. May he shine His light upon your sons and daughters. May they never leave from under the shadow of the Almighty. May our God grant you peace and promise.

Rest in the promise that:

"Thou shalt also decree a thing, and it shall be established unto thee: and the light shall shine upon thy ways." – Job 22:28 (KJV)

The Blessing of Abraham

Brothers and sisters in Christ, be blessed continually. I was thoroughly encouraged by this process. It was an intimate affair with the Holy Spirit. God Almighty, Yahweh, directed me during this process. He led me to an anointed and telling song by Donald Lawrence; 'The Blessing of Abraham.' Please note the lyrics and hidden message in this song. Tap into the anointing. Tap into your inheritance. God be praised.

I am the God, who healeth thee, Oh that you only trust in me. You are the seed, by faith receive the blessing of Abraham.

Wherever you are, where 'er you go, whatever you touch it's anointed to grow. You are the seed, by faith receive, the blessing of Abraham.

It's your inheritance, get your inheritance. You are the seed, by faith receive, the blessing of Abraham.

Wherever you are, where 'er you go, whatever you touch it's anointed to grow. You are the seed, by faith receive, the blessing of Abraham.

It's your inheritance, get your inheritance. You are the seed, by faith receive, the blessing of Abraham.

(God made you) the head, not the tail. Above, not beneath; a lender, not a borrower. Get your inheritance.

You are the seed, by faith receive, the blessing of Abraham. Get your inheritance.

The Gospel of Jesus Christ

And Jesus, when he was baptized, went up straightway out of the water: and, lo, the heavens were opened unto him, and he saw the Spirit of God descending like a dove, and lighting upon him: And lo a voice from heaven, saying, this is my beloved Son, in whom I am well pleased. - Matthew 3:16-17

"The time is here, and the kingdom of God is at hand. Repent, and believe in the gospel." - Mark 1:15

The gospel is that Jesus Christ died for our sins according to the Scriptures, that He was buried, and then He was resurrected on the third day. - 1Cor 15:1-4

He was delivered over to death for our sins and then was raised to life to put us right with God. By faith in this, then, we have peace with God through our Lord Jesus Christ, through whom we have gained access by faith into this grace in which we now stand. - Romans 4:25-5:2

If you confess with your mouth, "Jesus is Lord," and believe in your heart that God raised Him from the dead, you will be saved. For with your heart, you believe and are put right with God, and it is with your mouth that you confess and are saved. As the Scripture says, "Anyone who trusts in Him will never be put to shame." - Romans 10:9-11

That which we have seen and heard we declare to you, that you also may have fellowship with us, and truly our fellowship is with the Father and with His Son Jesus Christ. We write these things to you that your joy may be full. - 1 John 1:3-4

If the words of this book have affected you and you want to give your life to the Lord Jesus Christ; please pray the prayer below and contact a local church to begin your life as a child of God.

Prayer of Salvation

"Father, I know that I have broken your laws and my sins have separated me from you. I am terribly sorry, and now I want to turn away from my past sinful life toward you.

Please forgive me and help me avoid sinning again. I believe that your son, Jesus Christ died for my sins, was resurrected from the dead, is alive and hears my prayer.

I invite Jesus to become the Lord of my life, to rule and reign in my heart from this day forward. Please send your Holy Spirit to help me obey You, and to do Your will for the rest of my life. In Jesus' name, I pray, Amen."

Scripture Reference

Verses and corresponding translations used in this book:
Section: Declarations for My Sons
New Living Translation

- Proverbs 2:20 (NLT)
- Psalm 127:3 (NLT)
- Genesis 18:19 (NLT)
- Isaiah 54:13 (NLT)
- Isaiah 61: 9 (NLT)
- Psalm 144:12 (NLT)

New King James

- Psalms 112:2 (NKJV)
- Isaiah 44:3-4 (NKJV)
- Isaiah 49:25 (NKJV)
- Colossians 2:15 (NKJV)
- I John 2:14(NKJV)

Section: Declarations for My Daughters
New Living Translation

- Ecclesiastes 9:9 (NLT)

New King James

- Philippians 4:6(NKJV)
- Matthew 19:14 (NKJV)
- Proverbs 4:6 (NKJV)
- Proverbs 4:8 (NKJV)
- Mark 9:42 (NKJV)
- Isaiah 49:22 (NKJV)
- Deuteronomy 16:11 (NKJV)
- Matthew 18:10 (NKJV)

English Standard Version

- Psalm 144:12 (ESV)

About The Author

For over a decade Poetess Denise Fyffe has authored over 50 books. She believes her true calling in life is to be a writer and all else are bonus gifts that she has the freedom to explore. Her morals are deeply rooted in Christian principles, and she lives to be a genuine example of her faith. She leads the Revealing the Christian Life Ministry, which aims to provide guidance and resources for Christians.

She holds Dip.SD, B.Sc., PGDip.Ed., pursuing M.Ed., b.1981 from Kingston, Jamaica. Since 2001, she has worked in Education and Training, Publishing, and Information Technology. She enjoys research as well. During her career, she partnered with several organizations including Infoserv Institute of Technology, Heart Trust NTA, Pearson Education, University College of the Caribbean, and Prometric.

Potential. Denise remembers her teachers always telling her mother that she had potential; especially when her grades started dropping and they did not understand that she was simply bored. Today, this word sticks out in her mind. It is her motivator. She assured God that she would use the potential, promise, and purpose he gave her to fulfil her call.

Remember, "the heights by great men reached and kept were not attained by sudden flight, but they, while their companions slept, were toiling upward in the night."– Henry Wadsworth Longfellow.

Recommended Books

All books are available at online book retailers, including Lulu.com and Amazon.com.

Dear Reader

Thank you for reading this book.
It means so much that you have taken the time out of your busy
schedule. Nothing makes us happier than knowing that someone is
reading, and hopefully enjoying, what took us many months, even
years, to create.
Please stay with us on this journey. We welcome your feedback,
opinions, and suggestions about the book. You can write us a note at
Jamaica Pen Publishing on Facebook, or Twitter and at The Island
Journal website.
Again, thank you.

Don't miss out!

Visit the website below and you can sign up to receive emails whenever Denise N. Fyffe publishes a new book. There's no charge and no obligation.

https://books2read.com/r/B-A-ZOBLB-LOAID

BOOKS 2 READ

Connecting independent readers to independent writers.

Did you love *Declarations for My Sons*? Then you should read *Declarations for My Daughters*[1] by Denise N. Fyffe!

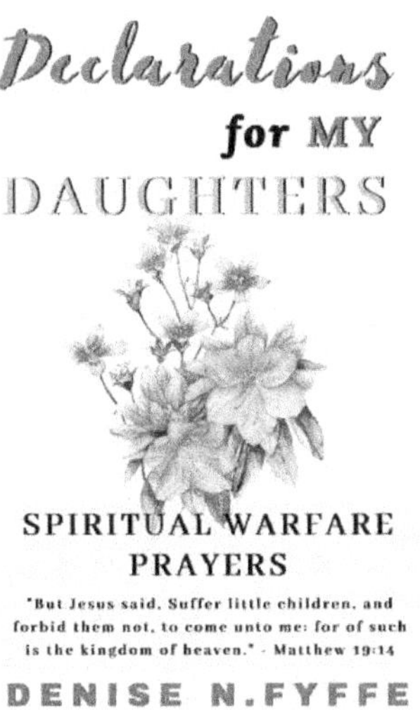

This book, Declarations for my Daughters, provides bold statements entrenched in the promises of God. The statements empower parents to decree godly declarations, which are good, pure, true, honest, just, lovely and of good report, over the lives of their daughters. The bible says that "death and life are in the power of the tongue, and those who love it will eat its fruits". Therefore, as guardians of our bloodline, we must take the reins and strategically place the power, authority presence and dictates of God, over the lives of our children; even to the 12th generation.

Read more at https://www.denisefyffe.com.

---

1. https://books2read.com/u/bx5qMk

2. https://books2read.com/u/bx5qMk

Also by Denise N. Fyffe

Career Development Book Series
The Philosophy of Education and Work
Sophie's Place: A Look at Career Development for the Disabled
Examining Career Development in Jamaica and Australia
Examining Career Development within Learning Organisations
The Impact of Learning Management Systems on Student Satisfaction
Empowering the 21st Century Worker

Declarations Book Series
Declarations for My Sons
Declarations for My Daughters
Declarations for My Sons & Daughters

Poetry Books
Recount Jamaica

Sudden Death Series
Tragedy in Chalky Hill

Bitter Exit in Kingston
Deadly Surprise in Portmore
Vengeance at Chapleton
Innocence Lost on Ken Hill Drive
Sudden Death: Loosening Foundations

Standalone
Be Lifted Up
Jamaican Pebbles
101 Jamaican Love Poems
Thieves in the Workplace
The Expert Teacher's Guide On How to Motivate Students
The Island Journal
Fibroids: The Alien Assassins in My Body
Be Encouraged
How to Keep Writing

Watch for more at https://www.denisefyffe.com.